To Ruth, this buik is dedicate

Acknowledgements

I SHOULD LIKE TO express my deepest appreciation to Professor Ted Cowan (Scottish historian and poetry-lover) of Glasgow University, both for contributing his erudite introduction to this book and for his endless patience with my frequent interruptions into his office. I am also deeply indebted to Robin Gillett for his wonderful cover illustration based on a canon table in the Book of Kells and to Alasdair Gray for his magnificent gesture of producing a portrait head of yours truly for inclusion in this volume. I am overwhelmed with the kindness of these men.

Credit is due both to Matt Ewart, who first gave light of day to *Møre-Sang* and *Turf Einar's Song* in the sometime art and poetry broadsheet *Skinklin Star* of the University of Glasgow School of Scottish Studies, and to Gerald Warner for his timeous correction of my understanding of the grammar of his native tongue.

I am pleased to be granted permission by Editions Gallimard to publish my translation from the original French of *POUR TOI MON AMOUR* by Jacques Prévert from his still-in-print collection *Paroles*, © Gallimard, Paris, 1949.

Special thanks are owed to the delightful Elspeth King, of the Stirling Smith Art Gallery and Museum, Edwin Morgan and Duncan Lunan for their constant championship of my poems, and to Tom Leonard for his kind remarks on their worth.

Finally, I am compelled to record my gratitude to my dearest friend Ruth Gillett, mother of Robin, without whose unfailing support this book would never have come to be written. I owe her all.

BRIAN D FINCH is a Greek Orthodox Glasgow Irish Scotsman who was born in Lennox Castle in 1954. His mother taught him to read and write before he went to Primary School, where he got belted by the teacher on his first day. This experience has coloured his attitude to authority throughout his entire life.

At the age of eighteen he joined the Royal Air Force. Within five years he purchased his discharge to 'regain freedom of thought, speech and action'.

He became a bus driver and was sacked from the biggest bus company in Scotland for opposing a pay cut in the letters page of the *Herald* newspaper. He gave up accountancy training when required to subscribe to an economic theory he considered untrue. Returning to bus driving, he continues to feature regularly on the letters page of the *Herald* where he proposed a private referendum as a means of subverting the Westminster doctrine of the sovereignty of the Crown in Parliament. He is now a Bachelor of Divinity of the University of Glasgow and intends to teach.

An avid reader since early childhood, he prefers verse with form, rhyme and rhythm. He likes stories, history, ballads and Dunbar. The poems in this collection reflect some of his wide-ranging interests. He hopes the reader will obtain as much fun in the reading as he had in the writing of them.

Talking with Tongues

BRIAN D FINCH

Luath Press Limited
EDINBURGH
www.luath.co.uk

First published 2003

The paper used in this book is recyclable. It is made from
low-chlorine pulps produced in a low-energy, low-emission manner
from renewable forests.

Printed and bound by
Creative Print and Design, Ebbw Vale

Typeset in 10 point Sabon by
S Fairgrieve, Edinburgh 0131 658 1763

© Brian D Finch

Contents

Foreword	11
The Economy of God	13
Jeannie Faa	14
Vinegar Squibs	16
Three Northumbrian Poems	17
1) Hymn	17
2) Daith Sang	18
3) Leiden Raivel	19
The Bantry Boat	20
The Breccbennoch	20
The Mother of God	20
On The Kellis Quair	20
On the Shelf	21
The Rare Adventures And Painful Peripatetics Of Ally's Tartan Army	22
Exhortation	23
Exegesis	23
Exit	23
Møre-sang	24
Turf Einar's Song	24
Sour Wine	26
Reflections	27
1) Communion	27
2) Consumption	27
Je suis désolé/Je n'ai pas une clé	28
On first hearing Carlos Kleiber's rendition of Beethoven's Fifth Symphony	28
Sage Advice	29
Wee Thinks	30
Ane ballat off Kyng Robert Brwyss maid eftir Barbour and callit Lowdoun Hill	31
Extra Vinegar	35

Ane Sang o Ystrad Glud	36
1) Strathcarron Fecht: 642 AD	36
2) Fute-not	36
Invocatio ad Trinitatem	37
Mains' Mane	38
Harvest Hymn	39
Snow	39
Christmas Eve 1999	39
Ossianic Fragment: I	40
Scotch Luve	42
Bleak House	43
For you ma dou	44
Two Julians	45
Picture of Sierra Leone	45
Simplicity	45
Raivel	46
Wee Further Thinks	47
How the russet dog wes maid	48
A Teez	49
Dinogad's Léine	50
Invocatio	51
Across the Causeway To Kranáe	52
The Experiment Continues	53
Butcher Beef	53
Skyooz mi Sun	54
Nyooz Fae Abroad	54
Willie Chisholm	55
Why (not)?	58
Oranges are exotic fruits	58
Come The Referendum [Yes Yes]	59
Greek*ish* Proverbs	60
Carmen Scotica	61
Deep Blue Senryu	62
The Glasgow Endgame	62
Shall I Stay?	63

Ex Aspero	64
1) cum editoribus	64
2) cum praetoribus	64
Three	65
Ethics, after Dunblane	65
Aye Ready	66
Social Skills	66
Silly Questions	66
Dancing the Cossack	67
Kulturkampf	68
Morning Prayer	70
Dangerous Drink	71
Ossianic Fragment: II	72
To Carolynn	74
A Song of Solomon	75
Desert Storm	76
On first looking into Viking Pingouing's Rhyming Dictioning	77
Quod Fearchair-a-Ghunna	78
Learning Difficulty	78
Partial-truth abortion	78
Fra Y Gododdin	79
In Memoriam Belle Stewart	80
Lines on Yesterday's Referendum	82
Pillow Talk	82
Morning is Broken	82
Glasgow 1999 Towards a New Millenium	83
1) Mission Statement	83
2) Progress Reports	83
In Memoriam Ned Donaldson	83
Maryhill Cross Morning Chorus	84
Quod Odin at Easter	84
Manifesto	84
Notes	85

Foreword

BRIAN D FINCH is a 'talker' of note in a city of eloquent tongues, whether in the convivial surroundings of Tennent's Bar or as the accomplished poet of this collection. He has an eye for the present and an ear for the past, a man much enraged by the bumblings of bureaucrats, the ramblings of the righteous and the daily inanities which pour from the media in print or on the airwaves. Above all he feels passionately about the obscenities of modern life, composing an almost public poetry in the time-honoured Scottish tradition, yet retaining throughout an outstanding sense of humour and an ever-present awareness of the ridiculous.

His poems reflect his range and his concerns, as well as those of the rest of us, whether he writes in Scots, English, Latin, balladese or Glaswegian. I first encountered his work in *Skinklin Star*, the sometime art and poetry broadsheet of the Glasgow University School of Scottish Studies, wherein his *Turf Einar's Song* seemed to perfectly capture the mood of the twelfth century *Orkneyinga Saga* in recreating the tall, ugly, one-eyed Earl Einar – surely a poet in his own right since his single eye enables him to see further than anybody else. Brian's historical vision of Scotland extends from St Columba's Iona to Anglo-Saxon Northumbria, extending from the *Gododdin* of Aneirin (the earliest poem known to have been composed in what is now Scotland) to the new Scottish Parliament, encompassing the Wars of Independence, the Forty-Five Rebellion and the romantic inspirational verse of Ossian, the Gaelic originals of which were as imperfectly remembered by James Macpherson as are his own effusions today.

Brian has a habit of dwelling upon failure, as is the privilege of poets – though it is one which modern historians of Scotland would eschew. For him there is a connection between the defeats at Catterick and Strathcarron and Ally's Tartan Army which infamously came to grief in Argentina, the bard paying homage to William Lithgow, the inveterate seventeenth century peregrinator who wrote much worse verse than Brian but who had a similar sense of the monstrous and the mundane.

In the following pages Dunblane is the horror which intrudes and which Brian handles brilliantly and with great sensitivity in *Invocatio*, to return to the theme in *Carmen Scotica*. As these titles suggest a powerful religious strand binds together the anthology which reflects news headlines concerning topics as diverse as Sierra Leone, the Gulf War and Mad Cow Disease.

There are echoes of William Soutar and Tom Leonard in this collection, but above all the reader becomes attuned to a kind of communal Scottish poetic voice. The past impinges on the present on an almost daily basis. At times it seems that history is almost as common a subject as football in the pubs of the Byres Road, for the very good reason that Scotland is an historical construct or it is nothing.

Here then is a clamjamfry of poems which draw on the past but speak to the present and the future. No doubt Brian will persist in his flagellation of the Establishment and his deflation of the pretentious. His tongues will continue to talk and we will all be the richer for it.

Ted Cowan
Professor of Scottish History, University of Glasgow

The Economy of God

Once this world began

Space to span began

Man

Then began

His outspan

Jeannie Faa

Jeannie Faa gangs big wi bairn
Til the heichest Stewart of aa
For she is but a tinker quine
He pits her out the haa

Davie Ross is but a herd
That keips the king's ain byre
An gies in-lye til Jeannie Faa
Ta cleck afore his fire

Jeannie Faa nou casts in strae
A shae wi lokkert-heid
But or she taks the bairn til breist
Young Jeannie Faa is deid

Our Davie snegs an knots the cord
He washes clean the bairn
Than he lays doun young Jeannie Faa
An merks her wi a cairn

Than Davie taks her guids an gear
Out-bye his maister's byre
Wi bangster cracks he braks thaim up
An brenns thaim aa wi fire

strae: straw; cast a shae: give birth to a bastard
lokkert-heid: curly hair; or: before
bangster cracks: violent strokes; brenns: burns

Than Davie milks his maister's kye
    An tries ta feed the wean
But no ae drap slips past its lips
    It prees the king's milk nane

It is about the mirkest hour
    That Davie wauks ta spy
Young Jeannie Faa tak up her bairn
    An sing a lullabye

She lifts the pap fra out her linens
    She pits it on his lips
An her wee bairn laps up the milk
    That fra her nipple drips

Than up an craws the reid reid cock
    That bells the crack o daw
As Jeannie lays her wee bairn doun
    An saftly smools awaa

Whan Davie spies the bairn is deid
    He plains up the cairn
Than he lays doun the span-lang corp
    Intill its mither's airms

kye: cattle (pl); wean: wee one; prees: tastes
wauks: wakes; linens: winding-sheet
smools: vanishes; plains: opens
span-lang corp: hand-span long corpse

Vinegar Squibs

Snow falls thick and fast
All our mountains look alike
Clean and bright – pure white

Words fly thick and fast
All our leaders look alike
Clean and bright – pure right

See fish? Fish is rank.
Juist twae thing's as rank as fish.
Yin o thaim *is* fish.

Three Northumbrian Poems

1) Hymn

   Nou hymn we heich   our heivenlie gaird,
   maister almichtie,   whase myndis thocht
warkis our wardfaither   his wonderis ilkane,
    alwaies oweran,   he ordered it sae;
    he firsten fixt   fowkis bairnteme
   heiven til housheid,   our halie lord,
   then midd-erd maid   did mankyn's gaird;
    alwaies oweran,   eftir thir daeins
   filled it wi fowk,   our faither almichtie.

PRIMO CANTAVIT CAEDMON
ISTUD CARMEN
ante circa 680 AD

heich: high(ly); alwaies oweran: eternal almightie
fowkis bairnteme: the children of men; thir: these

2) Daith Sang

  Fate unfoldan gars few or nane
 think as thichtlyke as thaim that maun
   thirsels consider suin the lord
  thar god sall gauge whit guid or ill
  thai did or daith, an duim its warth.

QUOD BAEDA
defunctus est 735 AD
CANTABAT ETIAM ANTIPHONAS
OB NOSTRAM CONSOLATIONEM

gars: compels; thichtlyke: clearly and unsentimentally

3) Leiden Raivel

  Wan fra wetwang,   an wondir cauld,
    out the innards   o erd I cam.
  Unworkit o wool-fleice,   weel I ken
  na heich hauncraft   o hair wrocht me.
    Warp unwaftit,   an waft unplait,
  nae thrumman threid   is threit on me.
  Nae shuttle-shaks   neid shoogle me,
  nor knock me nane,   wi nae loom-sley.
  Worms me wuive-na,   by weirdlie craft,
    o gowden guidweb   gleman sa fine.
    Wide as I wander   at will on erd
    heroes hail me   as halesom weid.
  Annoy is nane   thoch nou men flicht
    eager arrows   out thar quivers.

AD ALDHELMUM
post circa 695 AD

QUID HOC SIBI VULT?

wetwang: water-meadow; loom-sley: weaver's reed
weirdlie: uncanny; guidweb: silk

The Bantry Boat

Brendan steering, aft
Bearing Grace, crossing whale's race
Christ! Favour this craft

The Breccbennoch

Two doves wing above
The speckled hill – Silver-girt
Colum sings God's will

The Mother of God

Mary contained God
God who cannot be contained
Mary was big then

On The Kellis Quair

[folio 32v]

Thon dootfi portrait's
Nae dootfi noo, eh? – Naw, it's
Billy Connolly?

On the Shelf

In the Black Museum
Royal Air Force Debden
1973

Twinkle twinkle little man
Sing me sunbeams if you can
While I wonder why you are
Gently pickling in this jar

Plucked untimely from the womb
Swimming in this breath-blown tomb
No breath of yours will move a face
Or break the waters you displace

So twinkle twinkle as you can
You're no sunbeam little man
It seems to me you simply are
A homeless moonbeam in a jar

The Rare Adventures And Painful Peripatetics Of Ally's Tartan Army

['O wad some Pow'r the giftie gie us
To see oursels as others see us!'
It wad frae mony a blunder free us
An' foolish notion........
Robert Burns]

Hubris

Nemesis

Katharsis

These learns yese

Und so waren es

Hubris is what we thought

Nemesis is what we got

Katharsis is hardly taught

Exhortation

Black unblinking night,
Concealing right, veils my sight.
Lord! Unloose some light.

Exegesis

Can't you understand?
What? God knows. Words flow. Wind blows.
Jesus writes in sand.

Exit

Long-looking no more
Colum Cille leaves Howth Hill
Alba lies before

Møre-sang

Will ye gang til the islands young Einar?
Will ye gang til the islands the day?
Will ye gang til the islands Jarl Einar,
An never come back til Norway.

Turf Einar's Song

Came a king's boy
Calling himself king
King of Orkney
He kinged himself

Unkinging him
I killed him
Cutting
Splitting
His spine from his ribs
Ripping his lungs
Through the slits
Displaying them spread
Blood-eagled
About his ears

Offering to Odin
The folk-lord's fee
The duty due
And got
For my father's fall
I settled the scot

King Harald's lad
Halfdan Long-leg
Lifted his head
A kingdom to beg

His kingdom is come
He kings a cairn
It's kingdom enough
For Norway's bairn

Sour Wine

Haw. Whit's *bastard* Maw?
Wean's mither's man's no its paw.
Aw. Whit's *Jesus* Maw?

Wearie wayis walk
We gang. Quhence or quhethir? Quhy?
Quha kennis? We gang.

Quip. Be quick to come.
Quickly. Quell this quibbling scum.
Quiet quells the dumb.

Life is durable
While life is endurable
Life is curable

Lord tether the tyke
Let but ae sheip lowp the dyke
See the lave the lyke

Reflections

1) Communion

Lord
Sain our breid
an sain this wine
an thaim that eat
as thai are *thine*

2) Consumption

Kill it
Kill it deid
An whan it's deid
Kill it again
An than
Kill it some mair
Juist ta be shair
Or.......

Je suis désolé
Je n'ai pas une clé

Saint Paul de Pierre avait une pique
Il va aller *à l'*Amérique
Il est sur la plage
Dit: 'Messieurs, où suis-je?'
'Pour sûr, Monsieur, à Limerick.'

On first hearing Carlos Kleiber's rendition of Beethoven's Fifth Symphony

C'est l'empereur, m'sieu?
Mais non, m'sieu. C'est le dieu.
C'est ça, le bon dieu.

Sage Advice

And now My Dear
What seems to be the matter with you?

Ah'm black depressed
Ah'm stressed right through

I should consult an analyst
Or priest
If I were you

And you Good Sir
What is the matter with you?

Ah'm no ma best
Ah'm a wee bit blue

I should get pissed
Or kissed
If I were you

Wee Thinks

Zipping trouser flies
Ripping foreskins with the rise
Brings tears to the eyes

Swink skinks skill but swink
Whan skill thinks ta prink perjink
Swink aye skinks unswink

God gied Man hard swink
Aristotle gart him think
Auld Nick got the drink

Composers compose
Sublime chimes (*some* of the time)
Meantime poets pose

*swink: work, skink: crush, but: without
prink perjink: strut ostentatiously*

Ane ballat off Kyng Robert Brwyss maid eftir Barbour and callit Lowdoun Hill

The kyng lay in-to Gawlistoun,
Quhar nane durst hym withstand.
Schir Aymer hym a herald sent
To speik his harsk command.

'Gyff yhe wald ryng, then scowk na mair.
Turn yhe till nobillay.
Come undir Lowdoun hill Schir Kyng
Apon the tend off Mai.'

The kyng gert say, 'Be I in lyf,
And ye dar hald the vay,
Then undir Lowdoun hill, weill neir,
Ye sall me see that day.'

The kyng gert schar thrie dykis deip,
Thrie dykis deip and vyd,
Fra moss to moss, bot bar the road
That rins by lowdoun-side.

quhar: where; gyff: if; ryng: rule
scowk: skulk; nobillay: nobleness
gert schar: cut; dykis: ditches
bot bar: without blocking

The day did dawn a cleir cleir morn.
Sa cleir did dawn the day,
The sone did schyne on Yngliss steel
Full fyftein miles away.

The Ynglisch hors can host in forss
Thrie thousand men off mycht
Vith scheldis schene, in twa eschelis,
And basnettis burnyst brycht.

Nou gais our kyng in gud aray,
Sex hundreth thair besyd,
To steik the gap apon the gate
And thair his fa abyd.

And quhen Schir Amer them has seyn,
That war sa cant and keyn,
Come doun the hill intill the playn
He blast his trump bedeyn.

The Inglisch hors, thai hurlit furth,
Schir Amer in the van,
And doun ilk syd gaed stryd for stryd
Makdougillis cateranis.

*can host: assembled; scheldis schene: shining shields
eschelis: squadrons (echelons); basnettis: helmets (bas[c]inets)
gate: road, cant: confident (canty); bedeyn: immediately
cateranis: highland footsoldiers (ceithern)*

The Ingliss horss, vith speris straucht,
Enbrast thar scheldis braid.
Vith stowpand hedis on thai raucht.
Rycht to the kyng thai raid.

A! Mychty God! Quha thair had beyn
And seyn the kyng himsell
Vith valour gret that gallop brek,
Quhat mervellis mycht he tell.

The kyngis men, that worthi war,
Vith speris scharply schar.
Thai stekit men and stedis baith,
And nocht ane fa wald spair.

The Inglish horsis, reland sair,
Can flyng intill thar payn,
And can in flyngyng rusche thar fowk
And havock plaid thar ain.

The kyngis men apon them ran
And dang them hardelie.
Thai gert feill off thar fayis fall
Thai fawcht sa sturdelie.

*speris straucht: levelled lances; enbrast: gripped
stowpand hedis: lowered heads; raucht: charged
can flyng: reared and tossed their riders
dang: struck; feill off: very many of*

And quhen MakDowgill raxt the dyke
That wes sa deip and vyd,
He cursit sair the kyngis name
For he couth fly nor glyd.

Quhairfor he failyeit lowp the dyke,
Vith all his cateranis,
And tak our kyng fra up ahint
MakDougill brok and ran.

The vaward then did them vithdraw
Fra thar to-gret dispyt,
And quhen that rout the reirward saw,
Thai flede vith na respyt.

For sum war deid and sum war tane,
Sum flede vithouten scheld,
Schir Amer grat and tuik the gate,
The last to leve the feld.

Then lay our kyng all Cwnynghame
Full undirneth his hand,
As Aymer rade til London toun
To seik a fresche command.

raxt: reached; couth...nor...: could neither...nor...
vaward: vanguard; dispyt: repulse; grat: wept
Cwnynghame: Cunninghame (district in Ayrshire)

Extra Vinegar

A mother gives birth
To a single living twin
Two she could not do

Erratum

A mother gave birth
To a single living twin
Two she *would* not do

'Two from one won't come,'
She cried, counting zero-sums.
One from two sums one

Frost came late this year
Crystal nipped a flowerbud
Blighting little life

Ane Sang o Ystrad Glud

1) Strathcarron Fecht: 642 AD

    I saw a kin   o Kintyre braws
    Wi fire an dirk   on Falkirk caa
    I saw a twa   o tounsmen faa
    At Owain's caa   on Kintyre's braws
    I saw braw carles   come wi the daw
    On Donald Brech's kinn   corbies caa

2) Fute-not

Owain ap Beli ap Nwython
Wis king o Dumbarton
Or *Alclud*
In *Ystrad Glud*
Or Strathclyde
When *Dyfnwal Frych*
Or Donald Brech
An aa his braws
Cam to caa
Wi fire an dirk
On aul Falkirk

kin: host; kinn: head

Invocatio ad Trinitatem

Halie Auctor quell furores
Gar fragores wi fulgores
Nocht imperill we paupores
Lest we perish per tremores

Halie Saviour quell raptores
Gar latores wi lictores
Nocht indict we peccatores
Lest we perish per praetores

Halie Speirit quell livores
Gar actores wi colores
Nocht incum till our amores
Lest we perish per angores

Halie Triune quell risores
Gar censores wi fremores
Nocht dispyt we Scots scriptores
Let *thaim* perish per stupores

auctor: author (creator); furores: storms; fragores: thunder
fulgores: lightning; paupores: wretches
per: on account of; tremores: terrors

raptores: robbers; latores: lawyers; zictores: policemen
peccatores: sinners; praetores: magistrates

livores: feelings of spite, actores: dissemblers, colores: false fronts
amores: beloved ones; angores: vexations

risores: sniggerers; censores: critics; fremores: whispers
scriptores: writers; stupores: stupidities

Mains' Mane

The brattle's brak
It's dreyachtie nou
The caul kalens is gane
Aff the back o Benachie
Faur gorbels gowp an futrats falp
An fair gyaun growth's coman fine again
But Mains' beef are stappit aff the lift
Aa girsit braw black Angus nowt
Wi nae yin a spuingie-brain
The prognostick is flinch
The widder's brukle
I doot it's rain

brattle: bad weather; dreyachtie: set to be fair
caul kalens: unseasonably bad weather in late spring
faur gorbels gowp: where fledgelings gape
futrats falp: whittrets (stoats) whelp
fair-gyaun growth: vigorous new shoots
stappit aff the lift: banned from the drive to market
girsit: pastured (grass-fed); nowt: cattle
spuingie-brain: infected with Bovine Spongiform Encephalitis
prognostick: almanac weather forecast; flinch: deceitful
widder: weather; brukle: changeable; doot: doubt (expect)

Harvest Hymn

Slice this sodden sedge
Shake insects loose Bearded tits
Sing the scything blade

Snow

Cleansing angel-breath
Blessing Earth (beyond this hearth)
With silent white death

Christmas Eve 1999

Wild the wind's howling
About my bedroom window
Winter is jeering

Ossianic Fragment: I

My Love bestrides the summer hill,
Pursuing flying deer.
I hear the hounds' full voice resound
As arrows cleave the air.

By fountain rock, by mountain brook
Where rushes gently preen,
When mist adorns my Morven morn
I see my Love – unseen.

What voice is this the summer breeze
Brings singing to my ear?
Alas! Dear heart, I must depart,
No longer linger here.

The shield resounds. Now I am bound
To answer Cona's call,
And follow Fingal in his wars;
To stand, or yet to fall.

Should Shilric go, leave me alone,
The deer no more need fear
The summer breeze, that stirs the trees,
Brings hound-song to her ears.

Should Shilric brave the field of graves
    Beyond the western sea,
O stranger braves, O sons of waves,
    O spare my love to me.

If I should fall, build high my grave
    (Grey stones and piled earth)
To mark my name and mark my fame,
    And mark that there lies worth.

Let men recline at noon and dine,
    And there sing out my praise;
And you, Vinvela, do not fail,
    Remember Love's young days.

I will not fail, I will not skail,
    I will remember you;
Should death befall, should Shilric fall,
    My Love, I will love true.

Should Shilric fall, my fate will fall
    To wander winter's heath;
And silent rest my aching breast
    Where Love lies deep beneath.

Scotch Luve

The time is come my luve, deir luve,
The time whan I maun gae.
Sen Spring is here my course is cleir,
For France I steir this day.

Whit for ta France will ye awaa?
Wad ye juist up an gae?
An crack apairt a constant hairt,
An cleave ae saul in twae?

Than will ye quit yon cauldrife couch
The cruikit stick ta flee
An come awaa wiouten law
Ta aye mak bed til me?

I cuidna gar the aul guidman
Gang thole a cuckald couch.
Whit thoch it's true it's you I loe,
Ye pack nae pelf in pouch.

Than time it is my luve, deir luve,
'Tis time I wis aboard;
Ta seik in France gif thair's a chance
O luve I micht afford.

sen: since; cauldrife: passionless; cruikit stick: limp penis
wiouten law: without benefit of clergy (ie. in adultery)
pack nae pelf in pouch: have empty pockets

Bleak House

Father was English	Mother had her place
He never once kissed his sons	Quiet life for nice housewife
Father *was* English	Mother wore the face
Father travelled far	Mother learned to think
Light-footed lightly rooted	Little life for bright housewife
Father lived apart	Mother learned to drink
Allen needed place	Brian got his place
Little cheer from them I fear	Precocious child once resiled
Allen got no face	Brian broke for space
Allen gave them space	Brian would escape
Little cheer for him I fear	Little joy yet redeploy
Mother turned her face	Brendan* has escaped

---

* In August 2001, the author was baptised into the Orthodox Church with the name Brendan.

For you ma dou

[*Pour toi mon amour*
Translatit fra the French
o *Jacques Prévert*]

I gaed til the street o birds
an bocht o birds
for you
ma dou
I gaed til the street o blumes
an bocht o blumes
for you
ma dou
I gaed til the street o iron
an bocht o irons
o lourd irons
for you
ma dou
an than I gaed til the street o slaves
an thair I socht
but fand ye nocht
ma dou

Two Julians

There were two Julians
One was Apostate
The other sacked the Palace
Both spalded the state

Picture of Sierra Leone

Sallay Gobaa

Ex-Grandma

Hands

Chopped off

Tied

To her elbows

With *string*

Simplicity

OJ walks away
Nicole disnae walk away
Justice blinks the day

Raivel

Twa braw frog-horse are we,
Lowpand owre yon bonnie lea.
Freschit nane on aits nor strae,
Watter we winna pree.

Lang legless wull we hurl
Alang thae scoggie trails,
Until we staucher at a brae
Wee cuddies canna scale.

QUI SUMUS?

freschit: fattened; pree: taste
scoggie: sheltered; cuddies: horses

Wee Further Thinks

My hand to her knee.
Will she love me? What will be?
Joy or jail to me?

When Prince Hamlet falls
Falls the curtain too – but then
Saps will rise again

Would we make you sane
Could we cut inside your brain
Should we feel your pain

Could we make you sane
Should we cut inside your brain
Would you feel our pain

I would I could die
Should my time to sky be nigh
Could I die in I

How the russet dog wes maid

God and Sanct Petir wes gangand doun brae,
Heich up in Ardgyll quhar air thair gait lay.
Quod Sanct Peter to God in jocose vox,
'Guid Lord, mak this stane a reid lowrand fox.'
God tuik his stick and gaiff the stane ane brank.
Up sprang Tod Lowrie, a heland reidschank.
Quod God til Tod Lowrie, 'Quhar sall ye schift?'
'In the lawlandis Lord, thair lambis I'se lift.'
'Lift ane lamb Lowrence, thair thai will hing thee.'
'Quhattrack Lord off that? I'se eat or I die.'
God than he lewch and cryit his lamb.
He luikit ill-tane. Nae hoggie cam.
Sanct Petir seikit baith up brae and doun,
Yet nocht culd he find in that braid brae roun.
'I ferlie,' quod God 'now how can this be,
That I want my hoggie and we heir bot three?'
'Humf,' quod Tod Lowrie and turnyt about.
Drippit his gummis a gorrie flux out.
'Fy' quod Sanct Petir 'our breid can ye reiff?'
And fast fra a broum busk he hingit the theiff.
'Humf,' quod Tod Lowrie and singit the broum,
'Quhan schiphirdis scheip keepis, thai'se nocht gae tuim!'

gangand doun brae: going downhill, heich: high, air: earlier
gait: way, quod: said, lowrand: louring, brank: swipe
heland reidshank: red-legged highlander (ie. outlaw)
quhattrack: who cares, I'se: I shall, or: before, lewch: laughed
ill tane: discomfited, hoggie: young lamb, ferlie: marvel
gorrie: bloody, fy: why, reiff: steal, broum busk: broom bush
singit the broum: complained of injustice, tuim: empty (hungry)

A Teez

Herr Heine
Entschuldigen Sie mich*
Bitte

Ah hud me wanst a sonzie Mitherlan;
Wherr big oak treez
Wid grow so high, an Violet tip the pan.
It wiz a teez.

She kisst me wanst, in Scotch. In Scotch she spoke
(Man, did it pleez
Mi heir hur speik) the wurdz: 'Ah luv ye Jock!'
It wiz a teez.

wanst: once; sonzie: beautiful (sonsie)
the pan: the (her) head

*Gie's a brek

Dinogad's Léine

[A *Gododdin* bairnsang: *ante circa* 635 AD]

Dinogad's léine, brechan, brechan,
O mertrick skins is wrochten,
'Twit, twit, a-twitterand,'
I wad thrum, echt thralls bumman,
When yir dad wad gang til the chase;
Wi's lance asklent, in haun his mace,
He wad hisk the ratches rash:
'Giff, Gaff; hish, hish; fesh, fesh!'
Fra his currach, he'd kill a fish;
Lyke a lion, quell its brash.
Yir dad wad come fra the binn
Bringan buck, an boar, stags twal-rinn,
A brechan fraoch-hen fra aff the binn,
An fish fra out o Derwent Linn.
O them yir dad wad rax wi's lance,
O wild boar an lowrence an lynx,
Nane escapit that wore nae wings.

léine: smock; brechan: speckled; mertrick: marten, wrochten: made
quhisslan: whistling; thrum: sing; echt: eight; bumman: humming
asklent: aslant; hisk: call to the chase; ratches: hounds; hish: go get
fesh: fetch; currach: coracle; brash: struggles; binn: hill
twal-rinn: twelve-point; fraoch-hen: heather-hen (grouse); lowrence: fox

Invocatio

O Columba spes Scotorum
leva fletum infantorum
ab odio ab insano
serva domum liberorum

*Scriptum est
Ante diem tertium Idus Martiis
Anno Domini MCMXCVI*

O Columba Scotland's trewin
licht our fleggit infants' grewin
out thir daurins out thir saurins
ser fra dule our littlins' ourin

*Transcreivit
1/1/1997*

O Columba Scotland's saining
lift our fearful infants' graining
from this darkness from this madness
spare those dolefully refraining

*Paraphrased
20/10/1998*

Across the Causeway To Kranáe

[Not thus I lov'd thee, when from *Sparta's* shore
My forc'd, my willing heav'nly prize I bore,
When first entranc'd in *Cranaë's* isle I lay,
Mix'd with thy soul, and all dissolv'd away.

Homer
Translated by *Alexander Pope*]

I see no sign that here the tale began
(When Paris first put Helen on her back
And had his stolen joy) of siege and sack
For Troy, because a boy would be a man.

There are no signs that here he sired the bane
Of Troy that, after thirty centuries,
Brings me here, standing between sea and trees,
Seeking such signs of old lang syne, in vain.

And yet, behind these trees a keep uprears;
A bullet-scarred reminder of the years
That Zanetbey defied the Turk's viziers
Fighting for Freedom – and Greece. It appears
The Glory that *was* Greece* *is*. Why cry tears
For ancient piers. Greece survives scholars fears.

The Glory that was Greece: JC Stobart

The Experiment Continues

British beef was best
Eating nothing but the best
British beef *was* best

Meenister mou's mince
Meenister's dochter eats mince
Twa mous want a rinse

Sheep to cow it come
Sheep to cow to Man it ran
Now it's killed me Mum

Butcher Beef

Buy Barr's bully beef
Bully beef builds belly beef
Buy Barr's belly-beef

Skyooz mi Sun

Skyooz mi Sun
Aye Missiz
Whit izzit?
Much izzit Sun?
Much iz whit?
Soarri Sun
Ah doant git thi bus much
Much izzit furri bus Sun?
Hunner gran
WHIT?
Tae George Skwerr?
Naw
Diliviri iz extra
That jist gits yi thi bus
Yoo're styoopit!
Aye
So ah'm ur but
Ah'm urni alane
So Ah'm no

Nyooz Fae Abroad

Embra noo huz goat
A Ferry Em-poary-um
Glesca'z no surpriz'd

Willie Chisholm

O Willie's up, an Willie's out,
　　An Willie is awaa.
He's aff ta see the Chevalier
　　An Whiggish thrapples thraw;
But Kittie sits, an Kittie knits
　　A muckle saffron plaid,
Wi nocht a thocht on battles focht
　　For King or White Cockade.

Than by an comes a reidshank, boun
　　For France, an fell futesair.
'O whit's the news fra out the south,
　　An saw ye Willie thair?'
'Our day is duin. The Whiggish guns
　　Blew aff our micht an main.
The Prince is up, an on the run,
　　But saw I Willie nane.'

O Willie's up, an Willie's out,
　　An Willie is awaa.
He's aff ta see the Chevalier
　　An Whiggish thrapples thraw;
But Kittie sits an Kittie fits
　　The crimson til her plaid
As, deirlie bocht, a bluidie splocht
　　Besmits the White Cockade.

*Chevalier: Charles Edward Stuart, thrapple: throat (+ apple), thraw: twist
reidshank: bare-legged highlander; besmit: spatter*

Than by an come some horse dragoons,
    Bluid-reid the coats thai wear.
'O whit's the news fra out the south,
    An saw ye Willie thair?'
'The news is fine. The rebel lines
    Ken grapeshot is thar bane.
We learned yon Prince a prettie dance,
    But saw we Willie nane.'

O Willie's up, an Willie's out,
    An Willie is awaa.
He's aff ta see the Chevalier
    An Whiggish thrapples thraw;
But Kittie sits, an Kittie pits
    The sable til her plaid
For thaim that thocht thar honour ocht
    Thaim king the White Cockade.

Than by an comes a tinkler loun
    That's buskit fine an fair.
'O whit's the news fra out the south,
    An saw ye Willie thair?'
'Whan Prince parades as ladie's maid,
    But dout I do disdain
Aa kings an crouns an white cockades,
    An ken I Willie nane.'

ocht: compelled; tinkler loun: travelling man

O Willie's up, an Willie's out,
An Willie is awaa.
He's aff ta see the Chevalier
An Whiggish thrapples thraw;
But Kittie sits. Na mair she knits
Her muckle brechan plaid
For thinkan thochts on ane that socht
Ta king the White Cockade.

Than Kittie sits the tinkler doun
An brings sic fouth o fare
Ta stowe his wame an slock his drouth
As never wad need mair.
He tuik his fill wi sic a will
O meat an fish an grain,
He never kenned the cankert yill
Until he tuik the pain.

For Willie's doun, an Willie's out,
An Willie's shair awaa,
Thoch nocht ta see na Chevalier
Nor Whiggish thrapples thraw;
An Kittie rips an Kittie strips
The tinkler out the plaid,
The saffron sark an shuin o bark,
Whase ilka stitch she made.

*brechan: tartan; fouth o fare: amounts of food; stowe his wame: fill his belly
slock his drouth: slake his thirst; cankert yill: poisoned ale; sark: shirt
shuin o bark: tanned (barkit) leather shoes*

Why (not)?

Why is Pakistan
Muslims live in India
Who needs Pakistan

Why is Scotland (not)
Scotsmen live all through England
Who needs Scotland (not)

Oranges are exotic fruits

I'm no bog-trot Tim
Ulster-Scots with no Rood-rot
My forebears could swim

Come The Referendum
[Yes   Yes]

Why bring us this Bill	*That Britain will hold*
You have and you hold	*We hold as we will*
You tell and we're told	*We tell as we will*
You take from our till	*We take for we're bold*
You'd weaken our will	*Our will will unfold*
You sell and we're sold	*We sell who we will*
You grasp at our gold	*We're gilding your pill*
Why swallow this swill	*It's sweetness untold*
No freedom comes free	*What's free is just dross*
We're done with your dross	*You'll do as we fee*
You fear to be free	*We fear it will cost*
We count not the cost	*We've costed your fee*
We'll fight to be free	*Who'll fight for such dross*
We'll trample your tosh	*Just try it – we'll see*

Greek*ish* Proverbs

Five in the haun
Is mair fair
Nor ten an staun

Money mony
Wad wed

Spit at the sky
Spit in yir eye

Mony cocks at crawin
Ower lang the dawin

Het iron hauds

Hail hail
Drouth skails

The ass brays
The cock 'Big-heid'

Bites is better
Gied nor gotten

Whan the yaird isna weet
Dinna watter the street

Carmen Scotica

In Name of Father
In Name of Son
In Name of Spirit
Three in One

Protect our daughters
Protect our sons
Protect our babies
From these guns

Beseeching Peter
Beseeching Paul
Beseeching Colum
Hear our call

In Name of Father
In Name of Son
In Name of Spirit
Three in One

Deep Blue Senryu

Nae Hosannas sing
Nae *Deum Laudamus* ring
Nou thon thing is King

Deep Blue fear fall you
Deep Blue don't you think we're through
Deep Blue unscrew you

The Glasgow Endgame

Whatever happens
I have got a claw-hammer
And Deep Blue has not

Shall I Stay?

Shall I stay
Until the end
It may come soon
Or then again
Perhaps not
Until the rot
Erodes my bones
Liquefies my stones
And leaves me limp
With twitching limbs
With eyesight dim
And ears gone dull
With teeth just gone
My mouth a hull
An empty husk
My meat wet rusk
Dripping with milk
Dripping
At both ends
Or worse
A teenage nurse
To wipe my bum
Just like my mum
So long ago
And so
I say again
Shall I stay
Until the end
Or shall I go

I do not know

Ex Aspero

1) cum editoribus

Sirs,
Youse'll have had your tea.
Kindly return my verses to me.
Six months is long enough
To read the bloody stuff,
When you say you will respond in three.

2) cum praetoribus

Aye. Ah'm an 'Aye' man.
Aye. Ah've aye been an 'Aye' man.
Aye. Ah'm nae 'Yes' man.

Αυε. I'μ α 'Υεσ' μαν.
Αυε. I'ωε αυε βεεν α 'Υεσ' μαν.
Αυε. I'μ α 'Με' μαν.

Three

Who lifts the hills high
Who fills deeps with sky-born tears
Who drives the Sun's rise

Fruit of living tree
Of sun kissed vine – canker free
Quench the thirst on me

Wind I am on wave
Breathing life in leaf and tree
Griefless grinding graves

Ethics, after Dunblane

Is this *all* there is?
How may then we this condemn?
No! I say *God is*.

Aye Ready

I have a friend

Who bought a vibrator

Once

She used it

Once

It br
  o
 k
   e

Social Skills

You say you're his ex
With your kiss you keep his peace
Stupid drunk gets sex

Silly Questions

Is Venus female?
Is Venus the Morning Star?
Is Lucifer bad?

Dancing the Cossack

A Gypsy boy-child
Danced the *Cossack* baby wild
Doctor Joseph smiled

Women watched this child
Women who were unbeguiled
Not one woman smiled

Praising dancing feet
Doctor Joseph for a treat
Gave the lad a sweet

Women watched this boy
Weeping silent at his joy
Aching with the ploy

As the doors swung to
Doctor Joseph pushed him through
Up the Auschwitz flue

Kulturkampf

Excuse me
(Het boolz in the mooth)
Excuse me driver
Aye missiz
Whit izzit?
Whit kin ah dae fur ye?
Is this the stop for the Concert Hall?
Naw missiz
Luftwaffe Heidquarterz
Izza cupl'a stoaps yit
I beg your pardon?
The Lally Palais'z
Up the road a bit!
Whit's oan?
I beg your pardon?
Granted
But whit ye gonny see?
I-I don't have my programme with me
Aw c'moan hen
Ye must know whit's oan
Whit ye gonny see?
I believe it's a-a piano concerto
Great!
Who wrote it?
Tchaikovsky
I think
Tchaikovsky!
Hurray!
He's great!
Bit marshmallowy for ma taste but
Ah'm intae Wagner
Wagner?

Aye
Ah've goat the complete Ring cycle
(Georg Solti an his big-bang
big-band demolition gang)
Up in the hoose
Morse likes Wagner
Morse?
Who's Morse?
Inspector Morse
Ah'm soarri hen
Ah'm urni with ye
On the telly!
Aw — right
The television
Ah hivnae goat a television
No telly?
Naw hen
Widnae hiv wan in the hoose
Ah'm intae music
See me?
Ah listen tae Wagner
An drive buses

♩

He da! He da! He do!
Zu mir, du Gedüft! Ihr Dünste, zu mir!

♩

Erm
I-I think I'll just...
Get off here...
If that's all right...
Driver?

Morning Prayer

Father behold us
Son uphold us
Spirit enfold us
On this day

Peter before us
Paul to shore us
Colum restore us
On this day

Michael to shield us
Bride to bield us
Mary to yield us
On this day

Three to behold us
Three to hold us
Three to enfold us
On this day

Father behold her
Son uphold her
Spirit enfold her
On this day

Peter before her
Paul to shore her
Colum restore her
On this day

Michael to shield her
Bride to bield her
Mary to yield her
On this day

Three to preserve her
One to serve her
One to deserve her
One fine day

Dangerous Drink

Let us drink of the Drink of Erin
This cup is good for two

I have drank of the Drink of Erin
Good woman drink up do

I have quaffed of the Draught of Erin
Come darling coochie-coo

I am drunk with the Drink of Erin
Alone and lost but you

I have drained all the dregs of Erin
A bitter-tasting brew

Ossianic Fragment: II

On winter's heath I sit beneath
The sun, it is full noon,
While all around me silence sounds.
No bird sings out its tune.

The hill of winds no wind disturbs.
The mere is still below.
The deer have gone. The herd has gone.
Sad are my thoughts alone.

But is this she that now appears,
A breeze upon this heath
To stir up trees? O stir me please,
Vinvela, come to me.

O light of lights! O light my night
As bright as autumn's moon.
As noonday sun in summer's storm,
My love, dispel my gloom.

But, are you safe from death's embrace?
My love, where are your friends?
I heard that death had stopped your breath.
I heard. I mourned your end.

Yes. I am safe from death's embrace,
My love; but not my friends.
Alone of all, I did not fall.
I did not meet my end.

But you my dear, why are you here?
Why, in this desert place?
Give up your tears. You need not fear
That death and I embrace.

Alone, my love. Alone am I.
In winter's house, alone.
With grief I cried. Through grief I died.
I now lie pale below.

She fleets, she sails. Vinvela skails,
Grey mist before the blast.
Above this plain, I yet remain;
Of all my race, the last.

On winter's hill lies lonely chill.
Let stormclouds blast this mound.
Perhaps the gale might sing our tale
Of love and life unbound.

To Carolynn

Heid is as hairt
Breist as brain
Bide in ae plane
Bide wi nane

Plain out yir hairt
Skail whit's duin
O Carolyn
Let me in

A Song of Solomon

Adonijah
Beloved of Jah
Beloved of God
Is gone

Adonijah is dead
Joab (Ayab) is dead
Solomon is alive
May Israel thrive

A child trembles
All Israel trembles
New mother outfacing
True mother displacing

Adonijah
Prayed to Jah
Praying the Lord
Spare from the sword
The life of this child

The Lord smiled
Solomon wiled
Orphaning the child

Adonijah is dead
Joab (Ayab) is dead
Solomon is alive
Israel *may* thrive

Desert Storm

*[It was not sweet rain
On the burning Basra Road
That fell from the sky]*

The hunt is up. The hounds of Hell are running free,
For now. The mother of all battles is begun.
The skies rain fire. Black reeking smoke besmits the sun.
Flesh boils. Eyes pop. Bones, melting, point a bitter bree.
My gross Satanic foes (in electronic glee)
Obliterate my armies, roast them as they run.
'See!' they cry. 'See! Saddam is done! The war is won!'
Yet I survive. They've neither killed nor captured me.

The blast is past. My fractious foes are falling out.
Those that died deserved to die. They were all third-rate.
My strength remains. My Guards maintain my State redoubt.
Would they starve me out? Who would my Arabs berate
As Arab babies starved? Would Arab Mothers shout
'Saddam ordains this fate' – or 'The West feeds on hate'?

On first looking into Viking Pingouing's Rhyming Dictioning

[16.344]

Overcome with gaiety
Filled with thoughts of liberty
At the onset of puberty
Inflamed Hecate
Swore her maggoty property
(Redeemed from champerty)
Would end her carroty poverty
Eating un-chocolaty vanaspati
In Amravati
Or Ross and Cromarty

Then thought she
(Sotto voce)
'In *Scotice*
Sic slime
Neither rimes
Nor rhymes
Hauf the time'

champerty: illegal bargain to assist in lawsuit and share proceeds
vanaspati: vegetable oil

Quod Fearchair-a-Ghunna

[the Ross-shire traivler,
eftir the hospitality had displeasit him]

Peer farin gweed wyfe
Brunt bannies an brukken speens
Lyke fare thee this lyfe

peer: poor; gweed: good; brunt: burnt
bannies: bannocks; brukken: broken; speens: spoons

Learning Difficulty

Write? Ah canny write.
See me? Ah'm illitirit.
Ah jist draw wee trainz.

Partial-truth abortion

Make the skull break womb.
Break the skull. Suck out the brain.
The thing feels no pain.

Fra Y Gododdin

Nae lord at the lairdin
Nor slicht at the slatin
Nor mirth at the makin
Wi slugs at the sleipin
Wi knees at the raxin
Wi Earth as my dwellin
Wi irons my chainin
My knees restrainin
On mead-horn drinkin
Catraeth men's drainin
I, nocht I, Neirin
As kens Taliesin
Skilled in expressin
Sang the *Gododdin*
Or the day's dawin

QUOD ANEIRIN GWAWDRYDD
MECHDEYRN BEIRDD
circa 600AD

[Aneirin of Flowing Verse
Prince of Poets]

In Memoriam Belle Stewart

Belle Stewart's deid
The hairt bleids

The lass that sang
The muckle thrang
That biggit bields
An pickit fields
The Berryfields o Blair
Belle Stewart o Blair
Nou is deid

Nae princess Belle
Nae rank tae tell
By bann nor birth
Juist saut o yirth
A tent-born tink
Fae Tayis bank
Wi ninety-ane yeir
O sang an cheir

In Bellis kind
Scotland abides
Scotland remains
Mair nor a name
On onie map
Onie *auld* map

Belle Stewart's deid
Nou this nation
Hes its occasion
For teirs an greit

Belle Stewart's deid
Scotland bleids

Lines on Yesterday's Referendum

[for Hugh Trevor-Roper
eminent English historian
authenticator of the *Hitler Diaries*]

We've no history?
Then, were we born yesterday?
By some mystery?

12/9/1997

Pillow Talk

The language of love
Is insufficient my dove
Nae merr talk jist shove

Morning is Broken

Dawn glinting
Through glass dancing
Lightly shafting the gloom
Of re-knickering
With lashes flickering
Watched us leave the room
With just two words

How absurd

Glasgow 1999
Towards a New Millenium

1) Mission Statement

City of Culture
City of Parks — of Gardens
Of Architecture

2) Progress Reports

Provand's Lordship's shut
The People's Palace is cut
The *Burrell's* no but

Aa thae trees is doun
That stuid in George Skwerr – wherr nou
Bonsai bins abound

Tounheid Kirk's awaa
The toun council's caa'd it doun
Still the steeple stauns

In Memoriam
Ned Donaldson

Though Red Ned is dead
The concept of *Red* insists
Ned himself persists

Maryhill Cross Morning Chorus

Rosy Dawn returns.
Herring gulls girn. Bin bags churn.
The air (my ear) burns.

Quod Odin at Easter

Yoke-breaker, you bring
Tidings indeed. Out of night
Springs ring-spearing light.

Manifesto

Failin's no *faa doun*
Failin's *fail ta ettle up*
Aabodie faas doun

Notes

Three Northumbrian Poems (pp 17-19)

The modern Scots tongue is the direct lineal descendant of the ancient Northumbrian dialect of Old English, in which these poems were originally written.

1) Hymn

Cædmon was an illiterate (and aged) cow-herd when he composed these lines, the oldest known attributable verses in any form of English whatsoever.
When Hild (Abbess of *Strenæshalc*, Whitby, 657-680 AD) heard his tale, Cædmon was inducted and instructed as a monastic brother, thereby receiving a meal ticket for life.
Poets nowadays are seldom so highly valued.

2) Daith Sang

Though most of his works were in Latin, in Jarrow *in extremis* the Venerable Bede returned to his native English for these lines – in my opinion, the finest last words in all of literature.

3) Leiden Raivel

The original of this riddle is the Latin *De Lorica* (Of the Breastplate) by Aldhelm, which he communicated to the court of King Aldfrið of Northumbria by letter in 695 AD.
A later, West Saxon, version with a different ending is to be found in the Exeter Riddle Book.

On the Shelf (p 21)

On first entering the RAF Police museum, then at RAF Debden (1973), I expected to see the usual blood-encrusted machétés, plus souvenirs of *The Great Escape*.

While these were there, I was also confronted with an exhibit which gave me cause to think.

Extra Vinegar (p 35)

In 1996, the British press carried the story of an anonymous woman, pregnant with twins, who was going to have one child aborted because she was too poor to look after two children.

The media were immediately swamped with generous offers of financial and personal support for this woman, from vast numbers of ordinary people horrified by such a bleak tale.

It then emerged that the abortion had already ocurred – *not* because the mother was too poor to support both children, but because two babies would cause inconvenience to her lifestyle.

Ane Sang o Ystrad Glud (p 36)

The original of these six lines, appended to a manuscript of the *Gododdin* of *Aneirin*, is the sole surviving literary remnant of the ancient Brythonic (Welsh) Kingdom of Strathclyde – which flourished for several centuries between the departure of the Romans and the destruction of its capital by Vikings during a 4-month winter siege in 870-871 AD.

Following this disaster, most of the remaining aristocracy (the last of the Men of the North) passed down the Irish Sea into Wales.

They left behind a shadow kingdom, which was eventually absorbed by the expanding Scots of Alba, successors to the overambitious Donald of Dalriada whose defeat is celebrated here.

Raivel (p 46)

Nous sommes un Citroën Deux-Cheveaux.

How the russet dog wes maid (p 48)

Schiphirdis eit mair scheip nor al the foxes falpit.

Dinogad's Léine (p 50)

This elegiac cradle-song probably antedates the fall of the Brythonic Kingdom of *Gododdin*, or Lothian, to the Bernician Angles around 635 AD.

It was very likely transferred to Wales when the last of the Men of the North fled the ruin of *Ystrad Glud* (Strathclyde) at the end of the ninth century.

It survives as a manuscript interpolation to the *Gododdin* of Aneirin.

Ex Aspero (p 64)

2) cum praetoribus

In a recent Sheriff Court case, a witness was asked a question which required either a simple affirmative or negative reply.

Choosing the affirmative, the witness replied, 'Aye.'

The Sheriff informed him that 'Aye' in both Scots and English was *not* the equivalent of 'Yes', and asked if he (the witness) had understood what he (the Sheriff) had told him.

Choosing the affirmative, the witness replied, 'Aye.'

He was jailed for contempt of court.

Invocatio (p 51)

On Wednesday the 13th of March 1996, being unemployed at the time, I rose late, at around 9.00 am.

I did not that day follow my usual morning practice of switching on my radio.

At about 12.30 pm, I put on my hi-fi a recording of mediaeval Latin plainchant for the Feast of Saint Columba (entitled *Columba, Most Holy of Saints*) sung by Cappella Nova.

The Memorial of Saint Columba, at the end of the disc, consists of the following invocation:

Os mutorum lux cecorum pes claudorum porrige lapsis manum. Firma vanum et insanum *corrige. O Columba spes Scotorum nos tuorum meritorum interventu beatorum fac consortes angelorum.*

(Mouth of the dumb, light of the blind, foot of the lame, stretch out a hand to the fallen. Strengthen the weak and correct the *mad*. O Columba, hope of the Scots, through the intervention of your merits make us one with the angels.)

The disc finished at almost exactly 13.30 pm; whereupon I switched on my television to discover from BBC Scotland's *Reporting Scotland* what, if anything, had occurred.

I discovered that Thomas Hamilton had chosen that very morning to return to Dunblane Primary school and slaughter the children.

The same afternoon, I produced this Latin quatrain.

Willie Chisholm (pp 55-57)

On the morning of Tuesday the 14th of June 1994, while on leave from the Glasgow buses, I received a telephone call which occasioned me some distress.

Following this, I went to Tennents bar in the Byres Road of Glasgow, where I drank all day until I was thrown out at closing time.

I then took a taxi to the city centre and drank in the Griffin Bar (in Elmbank Street), until I was chucked out of there after midnight on the Wednesday morning.

I subsequently adjourned to the (now closed) Indus Restaurant in Sauchiehall Street for a curry, washed down with yet more drink.

Before I went for my food (drink), I purchased an early edition of the Glasgow *Herald* from the casino across the street.

I read the paper over my breakfast.

When I was finally flung out around 02.30 am, I returned home, finished the drink in my fridge and went to bed at about 04.00 am.

At 08.00 am I was wide awake, though I must have been clinically drunk.

For want of something to ease the pain (not from the drink), I picked up the property section of the *Herald* from the floor where I had thrown it, and began to read.

I discovered that one of the houses for sale, the *Chisholm Stone House* in Strathglass, has in its garden a carven stone whereon is inscribed the sad tale of William Chisholm, who went off to the Forty-Five and never returned.

Lying flat on my back, in bed, I composed this ballad in three hours — not rising until well after 11.00 am to write it down.

When I had done so, I felt much better – I have never written better, before or since.

Fra Y Gododdin (p 79)

This stanza has been regarded as a late interpolation (AOH Jarman; *Aneirin: Y Gododdin*; Gomer Press, Llandysul, 1990). Professor Jarman suggests that it is a development, in the direction of a saga, of Aneirin's earlier claim to have survived the battle on account of his song.

He thinks this is 'clearly not consistent' with the *Gorchan of Cynfelyn* where Aneirin states that he was ransomed for 'pure gold and steel and silver'.

I disagree.

I believe both statements can be easily reconciled, implying no contradiction, as follows:

The pre-Christian pre-literate English had no use for leisured prisoners.

Captives taken in battle would be ransomed if they were important enough, killed (either out of hand or as sacrifices to the Gods), or put to work as slaves.

If Aneirin was not known immediately on capture, death or slavery would be expected to be his lot.

However, if he then composed *Y Gododdin* while a prisoner, he would have revealed himself to his captors *as a poet*.

Poets were valuable people then, as the only human immortality recognised by the pagan English was that conferred by songs.

In short, Aneirin would have shown himself to be worth something.

Somebody would surely have paid a ransom for such a one.

Hence he would have been neither killed nor enslaved, but offered for ransom.

Professor Jarman then casts doubt on whether or not Aneirin even witnessed, far less took part in, the battle.

He says 'the question... is entirely speculative'.

One can speculate on anything.

However, *some* speculation *may* be sound.

In Celtic polities, poets were expected to attend great events such as battles.

Consider the Lordship of the Isles.

When MacDonald went to war, his MacMhuirrich bard always accompanied him.

At the battle of the Red Harlaw (1411 AD) Lachlan Mor MacMhuirrich Albanach sang the *Brosnachadh* (Incitation to Battle) before Donald of the Isles himself gave the sign to attack.

This was one of the principal functions of the court poet of MacDonald.

Yet such roles were not restricted to Celtic bards.

They were general throughout the North.

Arnor *Earl's-Poet* accompanied Earl Thorfinn the Mighty of Orkney throughout much of his blood-bespattered career, taking an enthusiastic part in many of his battles.

On one occasion however, he did *not* fight – when Thorfinn opposed both his nephew Rognvald Brusason and the King of Norway's fleet.

The result was sufficiently in doubt for Thorfinn to protect both his friend and his hopes of immortality in song by putting Arnor ashore before the fight became too serious.

However, this was regarded as such a remarkable occurrence that Arnor himself remarked upon it, in a poem which remains extant today (in the *Orkneyinga Saga*).

To conclude, I think that if Aneirin says he was at the battle of Catraeth, we have no good reason to dispute his word.

Some other books published by LUATH PRESS

POETRY

Poems to be read aloud
Collected and introduced by Tom Atkinson
ISBN 0 946487 00 6 PB £5.00

Scots Poems to be Read Aloud
Collectit an wi an innin by Stuart McHardy
ISBN 0 946487 81 2 PB £5.00

Bad Ass Raindrop
Kokumo Rocks
ISBN 1 84282 018 4 PB £6.99

Bad Ass Raindrop
Kokumo Rocks
ISBN 1 84282 018 4 PB £6.99

Sex, Death & Football
Alistair Findlay
ISBN 1 84282 022 2 PB £6.99

Men and Beasts: wild men & tame animals
Val Gillies & Rebecca Marr
ISBN 0 946487 92 8 PB £15.00

Madame Fife's Farewell and Other Poems
Gerry Cambridge
ISBN 1 84282 005 2 PB £8.99

Picking Brambles and Other Poems
Des Dillon
ISBN 1 84282 021 4 PB £6.99

Kate o Shanter's Tale and Other Poems
Matthew Fitt
ISBN 1 84282 025 1 PB £6.99

Luath Burns Companion
John Cairney
ISBN 1 84282 000 1 PB £10.00

Immortal Memories (of Robert Burns)
Selected and edited by John Cairney
ISBN 1 84282 009 5 HB £20.00

FICTION

Driftnet
Lin Anderson
ISBN 1 84282 034 6 PB £9.99

The Road Dance
John MacKay
ISBN 1 84282 024 9 PB £9.99

Milk Treading
Nick Smith
ISBN 1 84282 037 0 PB £6.99

The Strange Case of RL Stevenson
Richard Woodhead
ISBN 0 946487 86 3 HB £16.99

But n Ben A-Go-Go
Matthew Fitt
ISBN 1 84282 014 1 PB £6.99
ISBN 0 946487 82 0 HB £10.99

Grave Robbers
Robin Mitchell
ISBN 0 946487 72 3 PB £7.99

The Bannockburn Years
William Scott
ISBN 0 946487 34 0 PB £7.95

The Great Melnikov
Hugh MacLachlan
ISBN 0 946487 42 1 PB £7.95

LANGUAGE

Luath Scots Language Learner [Book]
L Colin Wilson
ISBN 0 946487 91 X PB £9.99

Luath Scots Language Learner [Double Audio CD Set]
L Colin Wilson
ISBN 1 84282 026 5 CD £16.99

LUATH GUIDES TO SCOTLAND

The North West Highlands: Roads to the Isles
Tom Atkinson
ISBN 0 946487 54 5 PB £4.95

Mull and Iona: Highways and Byways
Peter Macnab
ISBN 0 946487 58 8 PB £4.95

The Northern Highlands: The Empty Lands
Tom Atkinson
ISBN 0 946487 55 3 PB £4.95

The West Highlands: The Lonely Lands
Tom Atkinson
ISBN 0 946487 56 1 PB £4.95

South West Scotland
Tom Atkinson
ISBN 0 946487 04 9 PB £4.95

THE QUEST FOR

The Quest for Arthur
Stuart McHardy
ISBN 1 84282 012 5 HB £16.99

The Quest for the Celtic Key
Karen Ralls-MacLeod and
Ian Robertson
ISBN 1 84282 031 1 PB £8.99

The Quest for the Nine Maidens
Stuart McHardy
ISBN 0 946487 66 9 HB £16.99

The Quest for the Original Horse Whisperers
Russell Lyon
ISBN 1 84282 020 6 HB £16.99

FOLKLORE

Scotland: Myth, Legend and Folklore
Stuart McHardy
ISBN 0 946487 69 3 PB £7.99

The Supernatural Highlands
Francis Thompson
ISBN 0 946487 31 6 PB £8.99

Luath Storyteller: Highland Myths & Legends
George W. Macpherson
ISBN 1 84282 003 6 PB £5.00

Tales from the North Coast
Alan Temperley
ISBN 0 946487 18 9 PB £8.99

POLITICS & CURRENT ISSUES

Scotlands of the Mind
Angus Calder
ISBN 1 84282 008 7 PB £9.99

Trident on Trial: the case for people's disarmament
Angie Zelter
ISBN 1 84282 004 4 PB £9.99

Uncomfortably Numb: A Prison Requiem
Maureen Maguire
ISBN 1 84282 001 X PB £8.99

Scotland: Land & Power – Agenda for Land Reform
Andy Wightman
ISBN 0 946487 70 7 PB £5.00

Old Scotland New Scotland
Jeff Fallow
ISBN 0 946487 40 5 PB £6.99

Some Assembly Required: Scottish Parliament
David Shepherd
ISBN 0 946487 84 7 PB £7.99

Notes from the North
Emma Wood
ISBN 0 946487 46 4 PB £8.99

VIEWPOINTS

Scotlands of the Future: sustainability in a small nation
Eurig Scandrett (ed.)
ISBN 1 84282 035 4 PB £7.99

Eurovision or American Dream? Britain, the Euro and the future of Europe
David Purdy
ISBN 1 84282 036 2 PB £3.99

NATURAL WORLD

The Hydro Boys: pioneers of renewable energy
Emma Wood
ISBN 1 84282 016 8 HB £16.99

Wild Scotland
James McCarthy
ISBN 0 946487 37 5 PB £7.50

Wild Lives: Otters – On the Swirl of the Tide
Bridget MacCaskill
ISBN 0 946487 67 7 PB £9.99

Wild Lives: Foxes – The Blood is Wild
Bridget MacCaskill
ISBN 0 946487 71 5 PB £9.99

Scotland – Land & People: An Inhabited Solitude
James McCarthy
ISBN 0 946487 57 X PB £7.99

The Highland Geology Trail
John L Roberts
ISBN 0 946487 36 7 PB £4.99

'Nothing but Heather!'
Gerry Cambridge
ISBN 0 946487 49 9   PB   £15.00

Red Sky at Night
John Barrington
ISBN 0 946487 60 X   PB   £8.99

Listen to the Trees
Don MacCaskill
ISBN 0 946487 65 0   PB   £9.99

ISLANDS

The Islands that Roofed the World: Easdale, Belnahua, Luing & Seil:
Mary Withall
ISBN 0 946487 76 6   PB   £4.99

Rum: Nature's Island
Magnus Magnusson
ISBN 0 946487 32 4   PB   £7.95

TRAVEL & LEISURE

Die Kleine Schottlandfibel [Scotland Guide in German]
Hans-Walter Arends
ISBN 0 946487 89 8   PB   £8.99

Let's Explore Berwick upon Tweed
Anne Bruce English
ISBN 1 84282 029 X   PB   £4.99

Let's Explore Edinburgh Old Town
Anne Bruce English
ISBN 0 946487 98 7   PB   £4.99

Edinburgh's Historic Mile
Duncan Priddle
ISBN 0 946487 97 9   PB   £2.99

Pilgrims in the Rough: St Andrews beyond the 19th hole
Michael Tobert
ISBN 0 946487 74 X   PB   £7.99

FOOD & DRINK

The Whisky Muse: Scotch whisky in poem & song
various, ed. Robin Laing
ISBN 0 946487 95 2   PB   £12.99

First Foods Fast: how to prepare good simple meals for your baby
Lara Boyd
ISBN 1 84282 002 8   PB   £4.99

Edinburgh and Leith Pub Guide
Stuart McHardy
ISBN 0 946487 80 4   PB   £4.95

WALK WITH LUATH

Mountain Outlaw
Ian R. Mitchell
ISBN 1 84282 027 3   PB   £6.50

Skye 360: walking the coastline of Skye
Andrew Dempster
ISBN 0 946487 85 5   PB   £8.99

Walks in the Cairngorms
Ernest Cross
ISBN 0 946487 09 X   PB   £4.95

Short Walks in the Cairngorms
Ernest Cross
ISBN 0 946487 23 5   PB   £4.95

The Joy of Hillwalking
Ralph Storer
ISBN 0 946487 28 6   PB   £7.50

Scotland's Mountains before the Mountaineers
Ian R Mitchell
ISBN 0 946487 39 1   PB   £9.99

Mountain Days & Bothy Nights
Dave Brown and Ian R Mitchell
ISBN 0 946487 15 4   PB   £7.50

SPORT

Ski & Snowboard Scotland
Hilary Parke
ISBN 0 946487 35 9   PB   £6.99

Over the Top with the Tartan Army
Andy McArthur
ISBN 0 946487 45 6   PB   £7.99

BIOGRAPHY

The Last Lighthouse
Sharma Krauskopf
ISBN 0 946487 96 0   PB   £7.99

Tobermory Teuchter
Peter Macnab
ISBN 0 946487 41 3   PB   £7.99

Bare Feet & Tackety Boots
Archie Cameron
ISBN 0 946487 17 0   PB   £7.95

Come Dungeons Dark
John Taylor Caldwell
ISBN 0 946487 19 7 PB £6.95

HISTORY

Civil Warrior [Montrose]
Robin Bell
ISBN 1 84282 013 3 HB £10.99

A Passion for Scotland
David R Ross
ISBN 1 84282 019 2 PB £5.99

Reportage Scotland
Louise Yeoman
ISBN 0 946487 61 8 PB £9.99

Blind Harry's Wallace
Hamilton of Gilbert-
field [intro/ed Elspeth King]
ISBN 0 946487 33 2 PB £8.99

Plaids and Bandanas: from Highland Drover to Wild West Cowboy
Rob Gibson
ISBN 0 946487 88 X PB £7.99

SOCIAL HISTORY

Pumpherston: the story of a shale oil village
Sybil Cavanagh
ISBN 1 84282 011 7 HB £17.99
ISBN 1 84282 015 X PB £7.99

Shale Voices
Alistair Findlay
ISBN 0 946487 78 2 HB £17.99
ISBN 0 946487 63 4 PB £10.99

A Word for Scotland
Jack Campbell
ISBN 0 946487 48 0 PB £12.99

ON THE TRAIL OF

On the Trail of William Wallace
David R Ross
ISBN 0 946487 47 2 PB £7.99

On the Trail of Robert the Bruce
David R Ross
ISBN 0 946487 52 9 PB £7.99

On the Trail of Mary Queen of Scots
J Keith Cheetham
ISBN 0 946487 50 2 PB £7.99

On the Trail of Bonnie Prince Charlie
David R Ross
ISBN 0 946487 68 5 PB £7.99

On the Trail of Robert Burns
John Cairney
ISBN 0 946487 51 0 PB £7.99

On the Trail of John Muir
Cherry Good
ISBN 0 946487 62 6 PB £7.99

On the Trail of Queen Victoria in the Highlands
Ian R Mitchell
ISBN 0 946487 79 0 PB £7.99

On the Trail of Robert Service
G Wallace Lockhart
ISBN 0 946487 24 3 PB £7.99

On the Trail of the Pilgrim Fathers
J Keith Cheetham
ISBN 0 946487 83 9 PB £7.99

On the Trail of John Wesley
J Keith Cheetham
ISBN 1 84282 023 0 PB £7.99

GENEALOGY

Scottish Roots: step-by-step guide for ancestor hunters
Alwyn James
ISBN 1 84282 007 9 PB £9.99

WEDDINGS, MUSIC AND DANCE

The Scottish Wedding Book
G Wallace Lockhart
ISBN 1 94282 010 9 PB £12.99

Fiddles and Folk
G Wallace Lockhart
ISBN 0 946487 38 3 PB £7.95

Highland Balls and Village Halls
G Wallace Lockhart
ISBN 0 946487 12 X PB £6.95

CARTOONS

Broomie Law
Cinders McLeod
ISBN 0 946487 99 5 PB £4.00

Luath Press Limited
committed to publishing well written books worth reading

LUATH PRESS takes its name from Robert Burns, whose little collie Luath (*Gael.*, swift or nimble) tripped up Jean Armour at a wedding and gave him the chance to speak to the woman who was to be his wife and the abiding love of his life. Burns called one of *The Twa Dogs* Luath after Cuchullin's hunting dog in *Ossian's Fingal*. Luath Press was established in 1981 in the heart of Burns country, and is now based a few steps up the road from Burns' first lodgings on Edinburgh's Royal Mile.

Luath offers you distinctive writing with a hint of unexpected pleasures.

Most bookshops in the UK, the US, Canada, Australia, New Zealand and parts of Europe either carry our books in stock or can order them for you. To order direct from us, please send a £sterling cheque, postal order, international money order or your credit card details (number, address of cardholder and expiry date) to us at the address below. Please add post and packing as follows: UK – £1.00 per delivery address; overseas surface mail – £2.50 per delivery address; overseas airmail – £3.50 for the first book to each delivery address, plus £1.00 for each additional book by airmail to the same address. If your order is a gift, we will happily enclose your card or message at no extra charge.

Luath Press Limited
543/2 Castlehill
The Royal Mile
Edinburgh EH1 2ND
Scotland
Telephone: 0131 225 4326 (24 hours)
Fax: 0131 225 4324
email: gavin.macdougall@luath.co.uk
Website: www.luath.co.uk